THE
READING PEOPLE

How To Analyze People Like The FBI

By

Richard Martinez

Table of Contents

1. Introduction 3
2. The Ethnics of Communication 9
3. Human Character 13
4. Masks People Wear 23
5. Empathy and Compassion 31
6. Muscular Core, Posture and Breathing 39
7. The Heat of Conversation 49
8. Barnum Effect, Cold Reading, Mirroring ... 59
9. Persuasion Basics (and Wrongs) 75
10. Afterword 102
11. Disclaimer 108
12. Recommended Reading 111

1. Introduction

This book is meant to remove or at least dampen one of the borders between people, perhaps the most problematic border – the fear of unknown.

You know this feeling when you suddenly have to understand the people you have nothing in common with? For instance, you've got a raise, and now you're a manager. The pay is definitely worth it, except now there are people you are responsible for, the people you're supposed to care for and understand on the deepest level possible – and you consider yourself an introvert in certain situations, maybe even awkward at times, not really into talking to unfamiliar folks, not very interested in what happens in their impenetrable heads and personal spaces . . . what to do?

Or maybe you have to work in sales, and you know how to sell: it must be their thing you're pitching to the client, not yours . . . but how do you know *what* their thing is?

Could be you're invested in this topic deeply: could be you're studying public relations, journalism, sociology, or any other profession which involves what we call *a keen eye for human character* – or you merely want to feel more comfortable around the opposite gender.

This book will be useful to you in every case mentioned above, and a million more unique cases we cannot even think of now.

This is because this book is a tool – something to be applied the way you desire, to a situation inherent to your own surroundings.

This book is devoted to the analysis of observed human behavior in interaction with another human (you or someone else) or without. This book will not make a Sherlock Holmes out of you – this fictional character's skills are supernatural – but it will, if applied properly, make you much more observant, attentive to others, and – in case you want it – more influential in situations where judgment of human character is involved.

So how do we know you are usually open to new people, but feel introverted in certain situations?

How do we know you have a great need for love and admiration but you rarely show it?

How do we know you'd rather give orders than take them?

This book will definitely help you to find this out.

The analysis of people, how does it really work? Let's start by saying the process is extremely individual, so basically the analysis of people is a multitude of analyses of different persons. And this is certainly an art, which makes it possible to fake analytical skills somewhat, and pretend to be the specialist in it while staying rather unskilled. On the other hand, also because it's an art, you can perfect your analytical skills for the entire life, and pick targets matching your experience, being able to map and grasp the most complex and hard characters.

We hope very much you're going to use the things you will learn for proper causes. Many people who are supposed to be good judges of character – businessmen, HR specialists, journalists, project managers and top managers – in fact don't possess the required knowledge, or are unable to apply it. Many people call themselves "empaths", and yet distance from unpleasant feelings, or strong feelings, and don't connect with people around them all too well, preferring isolation.

Some people employ analytical tricks and techniques just to use the obtained knowledge for manipulation or exploitation of others.

This book is to teach you how you can feel what other people feel, the real empathy, something very simple to explain yet very hard to master for one simple reason: we're often not ready to fully embrace the perspective of another human being, share and understand their pain, breathe in their personal life and see what drives them. This book will talk a lot about remaining objective, restrained, and properly distanced as you judge another person's posture, actions, voice timbre, and so on – just because otherwise your own influence, your own emotional interference will bar you from proper judgment. The book's ultimate goal is, however, not to make you into a cold and calculative character akin to Niccolò Machiavelli – in contrary, we will try to explain why such behavior is counterproductive and gains you nothing.

This book's ultimate goal is to make you more open and more confident in your social and business communications on a personal level, able to know people, and apply the obtained knowledge in a meaningful way.

This book's goal is to teach you to think carefully before you act, and be kind to others in your choices and actions.

This book unifies the working knowledge of a few people, including a top manager, a UX/monetization expert, a behaviorist, and a free-time journalist. The experience described in this book is purely personal, yet the knowledge is practical, based on existing, and named, studies and research projects. The practical part of the knowledge found in this book is meant to be applied to any sort of situation, from a business meeting to a romantic date.

Yet first of all, this book is written to be brief and handy. So let us move on!

2. The Ethnics of Communication

The analysis of people is not a passive skill. It's not some kind of a special burst of attention that could be activated at will, after which it automatically tells you things about people around you, Sherlock Holmes way. The analysis of people implies normal observation, not supernatural zoom-in slow motion injections of private knowledge. The more attentive you are to people around you, the better you'll be able to analyze them, but this attention doesn't mean perfect vision and superhuman insight, this attention is more of what Bill Murray's character does by the end of *The Groundhog Day* – this attention means caring about people around you, noticing what they do, and what happens to them.

And this is a very important point we have to start from: mindfulness and kindness towards people. After you practice the techniques described in this book, you will learn to know more about those you will interact with. You'll know what makes these people happy, and you'll know what makes them sad. Basically, you will know how these individuals react to different stimuli, what makes them tick.

You may be inclined to use this knowledge, this special understanding of people, to manipulate somebody, to exploit someone's weak spots, to overpower their insufficient will with yours, or cause harm to them. After you read this book, you'll know that human conscience, <u>the knowledge of rights and wrongs, is merely a social instinct telling you</u> whether you'll be <u>accepted and loved</u> by your own kind for every consecutive word you speak and action you take. Like many instincts, this one could be dampened or even overridden with reason and rationalization. Many people do harm to others consciously with no morals to stop them, just because they know this will go unpunished, or is somehow sanctioned or allowed, or even generally approved of amongst their peers.

So in fact it's not your conscience that must stop you from using this book's methods for a wrong cause, but your honor, your knowledge of yourself as a decent, trustworthy, and caring person. Let's just finish by saying we're all adult people, and deep inside we all know right from wrong, merely by knowing how we wouldn't like to be treated ourselves; so the caution line is there, and it's visible at all times.

In this book, we will, as Sherlock Holmes would, put cold reason in the first place, and brush emotions aside. We will talk about the dangers of compassion as something undesired, distorting your worldview. We will praise logic a lot, and it may seem we talk about matters of the heart as if they are something lowly and primitive. This is not so.

Analysis of people is a research, it demands objectivity, it relies on logic and reason, so naturally, it is a task best done with a cool head on one's shoulders. Still, while applying the knowledge, always remember to consult with your heart first. May your deeds be as pleasant to those around you as they are pleasant to you.

We're all social beings after all, and cold analytical people are little fun. Just so those you interact with feel comfortable, never allow the methods we describe in this book overrule your normal human communication. Even more so, some of the techniques we describe will work better if your subject feels love from your side, or at least is unaware of your cold analytical activities, if they're going on in the background. Your correspondent being relaxed and feeling warmth from your side is always beneficial to you.

And always remember – by studying others, we know more and more about our own selves.

3. Human Character

Imagine a monkey carrying a computer. The computer is able to look around, think, analyze, and talk, yet is completely unable to move on its own. The monkey is free to run around, sometimes even where the computer points it to. And yet, ultimately it's the monkey who decides where to go, according to its feelings.

This is exactly how human consciousness works.

On the most basic levels of cognition, or, poetically speaking, deep inside – we are all wild animals, primates obeying certain primal urges and drives. Our basic behavior is instinctive – you know that feeling when you travel to work early in the morning "riding on autopilot" and only really wake up on arriving there? Or, how you become bored of *Tetris* because you start playing it without really thinking? This learned behavior all belongs to our primal core, our monkey carrying around our reason, the computer, which could be preoccupied with something totally different while the primate is riding a subway playing a primate-oriented mobile game.

Reason is defined very directly. Reason is the part of us that speaks. It's the part of us that either talks or converses within us. Reason defines where our attention and active imagination are currently directed, so while the primate is playing its mobile game, the computer may be actively analyzing someone of opposite sex sitting across.

Sometimes the monkey and the computer argue. Think of how a person trying to quit smoking feels. Their reason demands certain things, while their primal being may respond with an entire tantrum to get its point across, and who knows who will win in the end!

The trick is, the "you", the thinking part of you, associates itself with the talking part, the reason. And the reason is always happy to explain things away. Which is why, even if your choice and the actions that followed it were instinctive, done on autopilot, in response to some primal urge, your reason will still claim responsibility for them, and rationalize anything you chose and done in the past, then explain to you why such choices were made, based on logic. It will be done in retrospective, in hindsight, yet fed to you as something that truly and certainly happened before you acted, not after.

It's really important to differentiate between the things one does automatically, acting on a whim, without thinking slowly and attentively prior to it – and the things done consciously, after a true consideration, which would involve the revision of all possible outcomes, weighing them against each other, etc.

In his book *Thinking, Fast and Slow,* Daniel Kahneman discusses two modes of thinking – fast and slow thinking, as you might have guessed. This is exactly it. Our monkey thinks fast, it basically always knows what it wants and how do get it. It only turns to the computer it carries around when it doesn't know what to do, when it needs something difficult dealt with, things calculated, slowly and carefully – the way the computer does it.

So this is what you absolutely have to remember when approaching another person from the analytical standpoint: you're dealing with a dualistic being, the reason of which may work in two modes: either doing its job, or emulating it, letting the basic urges and drives pull its owner around, and then explaining to them why it was the most logical thing to do. Always try and observe in which mode the person of your interest is functioning at the moment: the reason mode, or the body mode? (Since primal urges are normally born of the body.)

This is where some religions find its concept of sin: their followers are basically required to always put their reason first, and suppress the cravings of their body. What happens if the computer tries to fight the monkey and subdue it? Results vary, but we can certainly tell such behavior is destructive.

Does a human being possess a freedom of will? This question is rather philosophical – is there multiple choice, or is the Universe linear, every state of it predetermined by the state that came before? We cannot know. What we can know reviewing every decision taken by us or someone else we analyze is, was reason involved in making it, or were feelings, "the heart" involved?

In practice, if a decision was taken more or less instantly, it will be an unconscious "lizard mind" decision, the choice our monkey made without consulting with the computer.

And if we look into our own daily choices, we'll see in 98% of the cases the monkey-made choice was indeed mundane, very typical, repetitive – perhaps inherent to this particular place and/or time. We know our monkey is trained to carry out this part of our daily routine, so we gladly entrust our actions to this "autopilot", and keep our reason preoccupied with something else.

But this also means our actions become more direct, simple, and predictable; our monkey is after all but an animal following a simple pattern of well-learned repetitive behaviors: brush teeth, wash face, use towel, go to kitchen, put kettle on. If there's suddenly an accident at this point, something's on fire or falls on the floor and smashes, then we're suddenly "back on earth" – the computer switches back from its screensaver showing distant lands, and quickly runs the analysis routine: what must be done? What to take care of first? At the same time, the monkey holding it may panic, and then the computer's attention will be switched to pacifying the panicking animal, taking control of it.

In any case, after the danger is gone, we suddenly feel more alive, more present in the moment. This happens because our body and mind both entered the mode of behavior we shall call an "alert" mode. This happens when our reason, our active attention, is concentrated on here and now, the beautiful moment of full self-awareness, full internal agreement, when as much of ourselves is under our control as possible. This is when we become lethal, war-ready, and totally unpredictable for an observer. What actually happens is, our reason, our common sense, takes the full hold, and the animal is happy to follow it into the fray.

To better imagine the two modes of action, the "autopilot" mode and the "alert" mode, we could turn to literary fiction: in *Strange Case of Dr. Jekyll and Mr. Hyde*, the protagonist finds a way to split his character into two segregated beings, one fully driven by instinct; violent, destructive, and asocial(sic!) Mr. Hyde; another a young doctor driven purely by reason – kind, clever, and righteous. It's curious to see the dualism of human consciousness presented this way back in the XIX century, back when primal, animalistic urges and passions in human being were considered sinful and shameful in society, and incredible restraint was practiced in social communication: you could only interact with another human being through a complex prism of etiquette, which called for your attention and involved long and complex actions, and speeches thoughtfully prepared, nothing ever rushed.

Then comes XX century, and Sigmund Freud, who calls the primal animalistic part "id", and the exalted being of pure reason "super-ego" (our ego, then, is like a slider of self-identification running back and forth between the two ends of this persona spectrum. Id still sounds a bit sinful, a Mr. Hyde of sorts. The soon-emerging school of Jungians calls the same thing a "Shadow self", and yet again, it sounds like something evil.

These were perceptions of specific times.

In our day and age, "staying true to oneself", "listening to one's heart", "following one's inner calling" and such being looked favorably on – seems like our inner, primal urges and drives were finally legalized, and in this light, we see Mr. Hyde is not really a monster – it's more of a poet torn apart by corporal desires, a being which represents our internal warmth, the love we carry inside – the qualities a cold creature of pure empty reason, the supposedly righteous and sociable Dr. Jekyll, doesn't really possess. People who rely on reason alone, and follow their personal gains while brushing emotions away, we consider heartless, cruel, cold, Machiavellian, and so on. Ritualistic conversations and pretense are no longer norms of society.

Seems like in our day and age, we finally see the key to personal happiness: the balance of both modes of action, a regular person staying in the middle of the spectrum instead of swinging wildly between the two absolutes, something XIX century's society was famous for.

Still, remember this while analyzing someone: in the "alert" reasonable mode, people act differently from their "autopilot" instinctive mode. Expect to see less patterned behavior when the person's reason is actively involved, or expect deviations from the observed pattern of behavior at any moment.

We discuss patterns of behavior in greater detail in the next chapter.

4. Masks People Wear

All the world's a stage, William Shakespeare said, *and all the men and women merely players; They have their exits and their entrances, and one man in his time plays many parts.*

This is of course true; and even when one individual acts as a different person in front of different people, it doesn't necessarily mean duplicity or pretense, or even an act. Your boss (or client, if you are a freelancer) is one person in front of you and another in front of their children, and this difference of behavior and appearance is a social norm.

It so happens we do wear masks, and many of us have to change their mask twice or even thrice a day – just to put bread on our table – and we don't even call ourselves actors!

Because it's basic survival.

And this is something quite important to remember: basic survival instincts predate everything in a person. They are the primary directives, the ultimate priority calls of the wild. There's a popular book by Eric Berne call *Games People Play* (this is a recommended read, as we even named our chapter in accordance with it) which talks a lot about role models, the patterns of behavior we love seeing in others – sometimes in a favorite cartoon character! – which we then copy and think of as inherent to our own unique, authentic selves.

One thing is definitely true: each personality is built upon this primal, absolutely wild, fight-or-flight creature buried inside each of us, the creature we become when we hit rock bottom, when we are reduced to our lowest, and our survival becomes the only thing we care about. Think werewolves.

Now imagine someone who, instead of a wolf, becomes a Chihuahua scared of its own shadow.

And this someone, who remains quiet and careful while at the brink, may turn out to have a much higher survival potential. You never know how someone's <u>survival mode persona</u> looks until you find yourselves together between a rock and a hard place, hence a wise observation of old: *homo homini lupus est,* which is again, the *werewolf* theme, the *Beware of Evil Mr. Hyde!* theme, which is not how it has to be, mind the Chihuahua!

A good manager or military commander takes mental notes of their team members' behaviors during a crisis, pretty much like a captain would take their team through at least one storm prior to real adventures, because this <u>"panic mode" personality</u> is what you want to know about a person you entrust certain things with.

Post-apocalyptic and survivor movies and books often display people driven to the brink suddenly becoming <u>paranoid</u>, <u>randomly aggressive</u>, <u>selfish</u>, escapist, and so on – but mostly the theme remains the same: as if a thin veil of civilization was swept away by this catastrophe or another, and you behold a human being's terrible true face, and it's a snarling grimace of a cavemen, or an animal of even more basic kind.

So this book of Eric Berne, the one we highly recommend, *Games People Play* – finds an interesting application when we are speaking of this borderline character, the animalistic side exposed, the Mr. or Ms. Hyde pole of the personality spectrum of a given human being.

If you ever read fables and think about the masks people wear, then you'll remember what the art of fable is all about: a fable is a human social situation played out on animals. And this is a very interesting observation, for indeed, this "survival mode" will often manifest as behavior resembling that of some animal: in a crisis situation, the person may jump at people and roar like a lion, or retract into a shell like a mollusk, etc.

Another strange yet beautiful application of the role model idea of Eric Berne: for human beings, especially speaking of cultural symbolism, it's very natural to mimic certain behavior of animals, or, say, cartoon characters they liked as little kids. We primates are great mimics, and, finding ourselves amidst the wild we will often unconsciously put on a mask of whatever crazy thing we think represents our true character best. This is the factor that could make horoscopes relevant – never ignore a person's Zodiac sign if the person in question *believes* in Zodiac signs!

When everything is quiet and boring though, when our inner animals are well-fed and fluffy – this is when they turn back human. And the faces of humanity are . . . yet again, according to Eric Berne, Erich Fromm, Irwin Yalom – the faces of humanity are shaped and molded by cultures through fairytales and visions of our childhood. Little kids watch life in all its many facets; they pick their role models from the heroic, epic characters of their childhood, and create their first romantic ideals. Will these ideals stand the test of time, or will this childish personality be swept away and replaced by a more practical mindset, picked up from books and movies for adults, or live role models of adulthood? Or, perhaps, the character of this child will be reborn in the streets, in the concrete jungle, each mutation of it a dose of harsh street wisdom?

In any case, through simple and direct social lessons, both lived through and seen/read about somewhere – the entity we call a human character, or a personality, is born, and by now we see sometimes this personality has more than a single side. Our society is still happy to present a single person with many roles that may require a totally different character, so we normally only become the true ourselves when driven to the brink. Only forced into the game of survival – or into any other primal activity, like a sexual act – the human being dons all masks and becomes a singular creature driven by basic instincts. We may safely state one may never truly know a person until this part of their personality is revealed, observed, and known.

And the truth must be said: the multitude of masks people otherwise wear is endless, and fluidity of them is extreme. This is because all higher level habits, so-called "social instincts" – they are learned instincts, and learned things could be unlearned in a wink of an eye. Someone may eat bread all their life, then hear about glutens and quit gluten products forever, which leads them to change their entire lifestyle, which ultimately turns them into another person, someone their relatives hardly even recognize – and it happens as easy as that, a small article on glutens.

All because learned habits are so easy to unlearn. Habits are easy to change. People tend to revise their life once in a while. Some of them do it every morning. You never know.

What we have to remember is, no matter how many masks the big carnival of society may force upon us, one part, this "rock bottom" part, always remains true to itself, hence the proverb: *A friend in need is a friend indeed.*

5. Empathy and Compassion

We all know what compassion is – it's a feeling of mutual care and attention found in mammals and birds but not found in many reptiles, for instance, found in rattlesnakes but not in tortoises or lizards.

Compassion is something we need to develop to become a good person to be around: it's your mindfulness of other people's wishes and needs, responsiveness to them (for compassion doesn't make sense when it doesn't involve action on one's part).

For the purposes of analysis, compassion is harmful.

You remember how Sherlock Holmes is normally portrayed – a rather cold and restrained character, even ready to risk the lives of the people he is supposed to care for in order to prove some theory of his? And it's not like Sherlock is a bad person – he can do little about this feature of his character, as it's only a side effect of his "deductive method", or rather, the reverse, dark side of his highly observant and analytical mindset. It's merely the nature of the game: a good analyst stays out of the picture to preserve it from their own interference, or at least limit this interference to the actions dictated by logic: *the criminal must be stopped, who cares if a young widow suffers from a PTSD as a result!*

This doesn't mean, however, that people analysis doesn't involve empathy. Quite the opposite: this analysis is *based* on empathy, or at least on something called "cognitive" or "cold empathy", merely because a compassionate detective sobbing and hugging the victim is of no use to anybody.

Let's refer to Wikipedia:

Affective empathy, also called emotional empathy: the capacity to respond with an appropriate emotion to another's mental states. Our ability to empathize emotionally is based on emotional contagion: being affected by another's emotional or arousal state.

Cognitive empathy: the capacity to understand another's perspective or mental state. The terms cognitive empathy and theory of mind or mentalizing are often used synonymously, but due to a lack of studies comparing theory of mind with types of empathy, it is unclear whether these are equivalent.

"Mentalizing" is exactly what we need; it's the concept that implies people analysis, detective work. It means the kind of insight into another human being that doesn't sway you emotionally. And these modes, affective empathizing and cognitive empathizing, are so different we could even claim they are mutually exclusive, or at least affection is something you want to restrain from while analyzing people, because the saying *love is blind* is very true, same as *blind rage* is.

How does it work? Imagine seeing a charity worker asking for money, carrying a sign with a picture of a traumatized child. Your affective empathy tells you: *it's terrible, to be this child. The life of this poor baby is sheer torture. It's horrible, what happened to this poor little thing. And this charity worker, such a noble person, doing such a righteous job!* And so, your compassion pushes your hand toward your wallet.

Cognitive empathy keeps you clear of these powerful feelings though. Yes, this child must have felt terrible when they photographed it. Yet the logic protests. How do we know who took this picture? And when? Is this child related to the money in the charity worker's box somehow? Is this charity worker a real deal, or is it a con artist who uses shock imagery to trigger people into donating money? This is something cold empathy is about, looking to understand another person's motives without being carried away by emotions.

Empathy has nothing do to with *sympathy,* although they are often being confused, and you see people who like to imagine themselves in place of someone else calling themselves *empaths,* although this is an absolutely wrong, inverted understanding of empathy. "Walking in someone else's shoes", imagining ourselves in the position of another person, is called *sympathy*. It normally resolves in us saying things like: "Don't worry, it happened to me a lot, it's fine", or "In your place, I'd go and see a doctor immediately." This way, we learn nothing about another human being, because we sympathize, not empathize with them.

Empathy is your ability to put aside your own self, your own worldview, experience, your own *angle,* and accept the world of this another human being, truly understand what moves them. How do we know if we truly understand another person? Easy! Remember how they say *lovers and fools think alike?* It happens exactly because lovers and *fools* empathize with each other easily, open up to each other the way their thoughts, feelings, and actions become synchronized to a degree they exclaim the same phrase in a certain situation.

Empathy is your ability to become another person and replace your own world with someone else's. It's like playing someone else on stage – except the stage is your imagination. How well can you empathize with me? 100% empathy means you can predict my words and actions perfectly.

Remember how a detective retraces the criminal's steps through the scene of the crime, touching something, pretending to drop something? This is about how his or her empathizing with the criminal would look – except of course there's no absolute need to move around in precise motions of the criminal, just getting into the criminal's mood and looking around the room would be enough.

Before you can do it in your head though, a good idea would be to practice it physically, learning *the dance* and its moves.

Cognitive empathy becomes possible because of mirror neurons: the part of our brain responsible for learning new behaviors through observation of another human beings (or higher animals), no matter if we observe them physically or review conscious mental images of them. We watch how it's done, we try to do it ourselves (mentally or physically), we fake it till we make it, and sooner or later we learn how it's done (creating new neuron connections) or abandon hope (and let the whole thing fade away). If you look carefully into this learning process, you'll see it looks very close to how cognitive empathy works: *copying and striving for a perfect match. Lovers and fools think alike.*

This is why, in order to analyze a human being in front of us, we must learn to switch to their viewpoint. It means we must learn to *copy* them, to *become* them, to *think* like them, and this is not a pulp fiction cliché!

To know one's enemy, one must think like their enemy – Sun Tzu, "The Art of War", a very ancient book.

In order to catch a criminal, any police detective will tell you, *you need to think like a criminal.*

6. Muscular Core, Posture and Breathing

The first thing we keep an eye for in a person is the condition of their muscles. Is the person tense or relaxed? How high the tension is and where is it concentrated? Is it a prelude to a fight or a flight?

The best way to find out is to copy your subject's muscular core state, just look at how their muscles are arranged and try to arrange yours the same way. There's a good expression, "to carry oneself", and your goal will be to carry yourself just as them. Your copy doesn't have to be identical, just close enough so you feel close enough to themselves – imitate them as close to perfection as your present acting skills allow (to be a good judge of character, a good analyst, you don't have to be a good actor, but it helps – remember Sherlock Holmes and his transformations?) It isn't hard – just contract whatever they have contracted and keep it that way!

Now, as we learned to carry ourselves like our subject of study, we must learn to walk like them and breathe like them, or at least pretend to do it, deep inside.

Much can be learned from a human posture and walk: people with bad eyesight recognize and spot their relatives and friends by their silhouette, their posture, their walk in the crowd of hundreds of people, alone, as easy as a person with keen eyesight would. Can you stand or sit exactly as your subject does, and feel as comfortable as they seem? Can you breathe like them, at the same rate, with the same depth, following the same intervals?

Try and practice it alone at first, looking at a video of someone else. Soon you'll be able to perform it mentally, running the process almost completely in your imagination. As soon as your musculature and posture *imprint* will feel identical to that of your subject; as soon as your combined breath sounds like one, it's time to analyze their non-verbal message.

Are they demonstrating the will to move closer, shorten the distance between you – or are they trying to distance themselves from you? Is their posture open towards you (face, chest, and groin unobstructed by limbs) or closed from you? (Folded arms, crossed knees, etc.) If their posture is closed, don't jump to conclusions: they may position themselves this way merely for comfort, not because they'd like to lock themselves away from you. If your object's posture is closed and is comfortable – they are likely an introvert. With extroverts, expect abrupt changes in posture, quick movements ahead (lean towards the person they're speaking to, or reach for them), meant to shorten the distance between them.

Body language is a nation-specific feature of communication – in some countries it's hardly used, while in the others two conversing people may resemble two windmills. Still, you can normally detect the heat of discussion by the amount and smoothness of gesturing, even when watching the speakers from the distance. The rougher, sharper gestures become, the less controlled they are, the higher the likeness of a conflict.

A conflict is something often provoked by the opposition, or a third party, with intent to unsettle us, upset us, or make us lose our temper and act out. Our goal in this situation will be to retain control of ourselves. This doesn't mean suppressing our anger or bottling our frustration. This means dissolving the heat of emotions in the cold presence of our reason. This means starting with controlled breathing, restrained posture, and slow relaxation of the muscle core, resetting it to absolute calm.

A person in control is not someone gritting their teeth, holding reins back – it's the person showing calm restraint and conscious choice of their words and actions. Remember the monkey and the computer? The last one is the analyst; the first one lives for battle, and spots a good fight miles away. There's a good use for this quality too: your instincts will tell you when the situation is about to heat up a bit too much, so your reason could be there in time to prevent unnecessary drama before it has a chance to happen!

The point is neither of the two parts of one's consciousness must be restrained or removed from the interaction. When the reason is cast aside, no civilized communication is possible: any conversation will quickly derail and devolve into something childish, silly, and virtually useless for any purposes but socializing itself. If the emotional part is suppressed, the person starts feeling discomfort.

This is a very important point, and it happens to be twofold: whenever you spot manifestations of discomfort in either yourself or your object, you will know it happens because the primal part, the emotional part, is subdued by reason. This may happen when the person's reason doesn't want to give something away, yet their body – heartbeat, breathing, perspiration – seems eager to betray them, so they try and shut it off using reason, forcing themselves under control for a period of time, after which their animalistic part will inevitably act out. You must have seen how, leaving the room after a difficult meeting, people will be overly childish and agitated, exclaiming loudly, pushing each other, craving some sort of physical gratification – it's all the backlash of self-control imposed by reason, now lifted.

Hence, to stay comfortable, to remain in full control of oneself – which is something you want to practice in order to become a good restrained analyst – one must never suppress their inner feelings! It's hard to give advice on how your computer could keep your monkey in check, as this is a personal thing, inherent to your own character. There's a huge number of venting and confidence-building techniques out there, and you're free to try them all! Just remember this simple rule: by indulging a certain whim of your animal, you grow it, not reduce it. For instance, aggressive behavior does not deplete aggression, in contrary, it increases your aggressiveness – same as being afraid will not deplete your fear.

Still, there *are* techniques helping you to drop the level of aggression and overcome fear, from the most basic things like counting to ten, naming objects around you mentally, or drinking a glass of water – down to counseling and transcendental meditation. In this book, we'll merely say the solution is out there, and self-control is essential if you want to stay an involved yet unbiased party.

On the other hand, this is what you want to notice in the behavior of your subject: not their controlled, reasonable actions, but their slips, their subliminal telltales; the small movements, expressions, and changes in posture that happen without the subject noticing. How to interpret this body language? The problem is, it's not only inherent to a particular culture, but also varies from one individual to another.

Many sources claim they're able to teach you some kind of universal list of telltales, enabling you to tell truth from lies, present you with recipes of telling an act from the real deal – but these sources are at best-generalized information, sometimes applicable to many people, enough to make it seem true, but definitely not to be applied to just everyone. The truth is, only your own experience, attentiveness, and insight will help you to read another person's body language, for there are as many body languages as there are different people.

For instance, when someone is trying to touch or hide a part of their face – lips, the nose, an ear – it's normally considered a sign of secretiveness, the telltale of a person lying or trying to hide some information from the listener. In many cases it's indeed so – and still, be careful not to call someone a liar just because they tend to rub their three-day stubble while they're thinking.

Another popular facial feature to be pointed out as a telltale: a genuine smile would cause crinkles around eyes, while a fake smile normally wouldn't. Yet again, in many cases it may be true – we often hear about "someone smiling while their eyes remain cold". Then again, the experiments show the "smiling eyes" can be faked more or less easily, and if you were to encounter a sociopathic person, someone good at mimicry – you'd never catch them faking a smile. (We'll talk about spotting such individuals in Chapter 8.)

Approach tendencies in the posture of your subject may mean aggression – or they could mean affection, and only your judgment may discern between the two. If your subject demonstrates avoidance tendencies – this, yet again, could mean an entire spectrum of emotions: apathy, fear, disgust, mistrust, submission, meekness, and so on.

A good analyst would always view the non-verbal signals of their subject as a part of the bigger picture, applying to them the knowledge of this person as a whole. Even a habit as simple as biting one's fingernails – are you sure I bite mine when I'm nervous? It may happen a person tends to stick their thumb in their mouth while they're thoughtful, relaxed, their attention directed inward – miles from feeling nervous!

Always remember: what you see is only half of the picture. Another half, no less important, is what you hear.

7. The Heat of Conversation

Spoken language is an extremely powerful tool. Ants, bees, and birds may be far better builders than us humans, and a simple flower could be more beautiful than an artwork of a genius painter, and still, it's the ability to formulate our thoughts in words that set us apart from the rest of nature. Thanks to spoken language, we human beings may by right call ourselves the only creatures on Earth able not only to collect information, but also to store it, organize it, and pass it on to other humans. Words are powerful, and they certainly could kill.

And still, before we even concern ourselves with them and their meaning, we're going to listen for something else, something we could do before we could even speak. A poet could have called it the *songs people sing.*

Picture a two-year-old child, not yet able to speak a single word. Still, it's able to get its point across by the intonation only! All it can do is hum and moan, and yet, our child is capable of humming and moaning in a hundred different ways, and many of its intonations are so universal and primordial, we don't need the child's mother to interpret for us – in 99% of cases, we are able to tell what the child wants to say just because we can, because the baby cooing language is pretty much universal!

Ask any professional negotiator, be it a diplomat, a manager, an HR, or a salesperson – while waiting for the other party to respond, what exactly they anticipate the most, where their attention is concentrated? You'll hear a unanimous "it's not *what* they say – it's *how* they say it".

Remember how the most basic, primal part of the human character always acts first? By listening to intonation, we hear the voice of this very part of the speaker, their instinctive side. What matters here first is emotional involvement: how short are the pauses before your subject's answers? If your subject responds to verbal remarks addressed to them almost immediately, taking no time to employ reason, you can be sure their feelings are very much involved. Expect the answers of your subject to be passionate, biased, and loaded with emotion. In this state, a person tends to say things they wouldn't part with otherwise – be sure not to miss anything important from the information being delivered!

If pauses before their answers are long, this could happen for two reasons: either your subject's answers are less emotional, well-prepared, tested and weighed mentally, and employ as much common sense (slow thinking) as possible – or your subject is unsure of what to say. Yet again, listen to the intonation and voice timbre to understand which case you are dealing with. Is the speaker's voice confident, solid, and flat – or is their intonation of a shaky, roaming, ever-changing kind? Imagine the air column inside the speaker's lungs – the physical volume of air inside their lungs and throat. Is it stable, well-measured, and carefully replenished by breathing, or is it unsteady and erratic, often making your subject hyperventilate or lose breath?

And yet again, speaking of interpretation of your findings – everything about a particular human being is personal, and every particular individual is, well, individual. Same as we don't recommend using pop-psychological "detective work" on your subject's posture, muscular core, and breathing – the same way, applying all kinds of generalized pigeon-hole labeling to your subject's intonations will inevitably cause fundamental errors in your judgment.

Yes, we could say if the speaker's intonation is weak, shaky, and rambling, it may speak of their uncertainty, lack of knowledge, perhaps even their weak attempt at lies! Except in some people, it's their normal voice timbre. When your subject takes a big pause and makes a thoughtful face – does it mean they're really thinking on what to say next, or it's just their concept of polite and intelligent conversation, during which they're *supposed* to act this way? Yet again, it's very individual.

Speaking of truth and lies, all you need to know to be able to discern one from another is, lying involves imagination, while telling truth only involves remembering. What does it tell us?

First of all, imagination involves some brain work, and if the person in question doesn't use their imagination professionally on regular basis – like an artist or a con man would do – then we definitely shall expect a longer pause before the answer is given, perhaps hear a change in voice timbre or spot minor changes in the facial expression. An inexperienced liar will also try to avoid eye contact, blush, or sweat excessively.

If the lie was prepackaged however, and the person practiced its delivery prior to the conversation, it could come so fast it's going to be *too* fast. If the expected answer was supposed to involve reason, slow thinking – and it came straight off, like something instinctive – there's a high chance the answer was prepackaged, and on closer examination the information provided may prove to be untrue.

Untrue – or just a mess, a jumble of fact and fiction, a biased rationalization, a bout of wishful thinking? How do we tell?

The only way we can tell is by listening carefully, memorizing our findings, learning more and more about this particular individual.

And this is a very important point. In the next chapter, we will review several active analytical techniques, something you can say or ask in a conversation to quickly find out important details about your subject's character. We will no longer remain a silent observer – and this is where danger lies!

Many of us love to talk. Many of us enjoy listening to ourselves in a conversation. Some of us tend to ignore the bulk of what was said by someone else, as our own pleasant and elegant phrasing, our own rhetorical prowess drowns out everything else. This is especially true for beginner psychologists (or people who read up on psychology): they are so sure of their own claims they even forget to match them against the actual individual they're talking to. Many of the books these people read provide them with easy answers: this one is an extrovert, this one an introvert. This person is a subtype 2 of type A, while this one is a subtype 1 of type B. It's so hard to listen and observe patiently when you can just make statements and point fingers instead!

And yet, all theoretical knowledge, no matter if false or true, is useless without the proper practical mindset. You can cover your subject with labels and categories from head to toes, and yet learn nothing about them. Or even worse, you can develop a whole wrong picture of them, backed up by tons of material you read, and even the practical, observed evidence will be unable to sway you from your firm yet wrong belief.

To make sure this won't happen, always remember: you are the analyst! Not the other person who wrote the book. Not the book itself. No matter how much you read, it's nothing but your own perception, your own knowledge of this particular individual that will tell you what's really going on inside their head. If the person in front of you is someone new, someone you hadn't studied well yet, no amount of theoretical knowledge will help you close the gap – only the practical observation and communication will ensure you know as much about your subject as it's possible to know.

What if you're bad at noticing things, easily distracted, not really observant? Let's just say it works like muscle! The analytical skill is not a superpower you will obtain on reading this book. It's something we discover in ourselves and develop! The more you practice analysis, the better at analysis you become, so make it a habit.

Whenever you're free, and there are many unfamiliar subjects in front of you, switch the scanning mode on! Try and figure out things about people around you. Whenever you're lost and don't know what to look at, use cognitive empathy. Tell yourself: I am this person now. Who am I? How do I feel? What am I going to do or say next? The better you're at this, the more confident you will feel about your predictions and the higher correlation of them and actual reality you will observe. Even better – by becoming more attentive to others, more eager to watch and listen, showing more interest in people around you, you will become much more pleasant company! We all like it when people notice our new haircut. When someone notices what's happening inside of us and offers their attention in response – it could be enough for us to fall in love.

Up to now, we were speaking about passive observation only. In the next chapter, we will finally discuss the active methods of analysis, the things you could say and do to find out more about somebody. But the fact remains: when the observer enters the picture, the picture will inevitably change. Only use the active methods if you cannot afford passive learning! Remember what Al Pacino said in his famous speech in *The Devil's Advocate?* "Free will, it's like butterfly wings – once touched, they never get off the ground."

Remember an old saying about how we've got two ears and one mouth, so we should listen twice and talk once? We'll go as far as tell you to *listen always and only talk when it's needed.*

8. Barnum Effect, Cold Reading, Mirroring

Let's say plain observation doesn't help anymore. It may happen we learned everything we could from our subject while observing them passively, and no new information may possibly be obtained. Or, could be our time is limited, and we need to get to know the subject quickly, in a matter of minutes. When this happens, we cannot afford to stay a passive observer – we have to act!

The worst thing you can do in this case is resort to interrogation. Be it a job interview, a TV show, or a romantic date – subjecting the person of your interest in a line of tedious pre-fabricated questions will bore them out really quickly. If you read the previous chapters carefully, and your observational habits are in place, then you'll notice after only a few questions your subject will become aloof, unwilling, demotivated, and so on. We all hate answering plain questions about our character, and when asked to "name 5 of your worst qualities" we can even get angry with the interviewer. *How is it even their business?* It's a very effective way to terminate your warm, humane relations with someone – to give them a blank to fill, bore them to tears, and then intrude into their personal space in such an aggressive manner.

Wouldn't it be better to open our active analysis with letting the person in question know we do understand them, can identify with them, see what they are and appreciate it? How do we open our conversation then, and what do we say to instantly break the ice and predispose the person towards us?

Here we must turn to trick fortune tellers and mediums use; the trick that may give you a hint why horoscopes and Tarot readings seem to work although they don't make sense scientifically.

This trick is called a *Barnum effect,* also known as *Forer effect,* named either in honor of a famous showman Phineas Barnum, the first registered user of so-called "Barnum statements", which he employed in order to "telepathically read" his audience members – or after an American psychologist Bertram Forer, who analyzed the psychological mechanisms behind said "telepathy" and recreated the situation experimentally. What he did was offer each of his students a "unique personality evaluation chart" consisting entirely of the statements which seem personal, yet in fact apply to pretty much anyone. The students were asked to evaluate the accuracy of every statement as applied to their character – and the correlation points were incredibly high, *4.7 out of 5* being the median, despite the fact every student received exactly the same set of statements, for instance:

- *You have a tendency to be critical of yourself;*

- *Some of your aspirations tend to be pretty unrealistic;*

- At times you are extroverted, affable, sociable, while at other times you are introverted, wary, reserved;

- While you have some personality weaknesses, you are generally able to compensate for them, etc.

Said Barnum effect is a perfect initial step in a conversation during which you intend to obtain close knowledge of your subject. Remember those personal questions from our introduction?

How do we know you are usually open to new people, but feel introverted in certain situations?

We know it because it applies to pretty much everyone. Doesn't it?

How do we know you have a great need for love and admiration but you rarely show it?

Same thing. Isn't it?

How do we know you'd rather give orders than take them?

This one is tricky; of course some people lack initiative, and they'd rather take orders and worry about nothing . . . the question is, would such a person be reading a book on analysis of people? And the sure bet is, no, they wouldn't.

One of the reasons why the Barnum effect works, besides the generalized statements, is something called a *confirmation bias*. It claims we tend to agree with descriptions of our character *if we like them*, not because of them being true. Maybe you do show a need for admiration – you could be needy and even narcissistic for all we know! – and yet, who would disagree with someone calling them reserved, confident, a strong and silent type? It takes certain courage and objectivity, disagreeing with a good thing said about ourselves – so normally, we tend to agree.

Where is the analysis though? What we were speaking about until now is related to establishing contact, breaking the ice. Of what use to us is someone's "yes" said in response to a Barnum statement?

The analysis begins when we continue the discourse and narrow things down; zoom in on certain qualities of the subject's character that interest us. This technique is called *cold reading* ("cold" means you're honestly unfamiliar with your subject) and it's employed equally often by salesmen, show businessmen, journalists, and con artists.

It helps you study your subject while pretending to know them well from the start. This way, the conversation is much warmer. In fact you can regulate the warmth by interchanging ego-pleasing confirmation-biased remarks, then offering critical judgment in a reasonable and "sobering" manner, finding out actual new information about the subject. Let's see how Susan interviews Mark for the job.

Susan: "Please tell me how high your skill level is."

Mark: "I'm a senior specialist."

Susan: "Do you know Python? And C++?"

Mark: "Yes, I do, I'm familiar with both."

Susan: "Are you also familiar with MySQL?"

Mark: "Yes."

Susan: "What are five good qualities of yours you could name?"

Mark: "Well, I'm reliable, I'm highly skilled, I'm a team player, I have good learning skills and good leadership skills . . ."

Susan: "Okay, now please name . . . let's say three your worst qualities?"

Mark: "Well, I wake up early, not many people like it."

Susan: "Yes, I'm an owl."

Mark: "Yes. I also snore."

Susan: "Oh" *laughs*

Mark: *laughs*

Susan: "Well, the test you did at home also seems done well, so congratulations, welcome aboard!"

This specialist is rather naïve of course, yet the root of all evil lies in her offering Mark to fill the blanks rather than establishing personal contact and then analyzing him quickly, actively, and effectively. Let's see how Megan does the job.

Megan: "Hello, Mark."

Mark: "Hello."

Megan: "I can see you're an open-minded person, yet sometimes you feel locked up . . . like maybe now? Is this so?"

Mark: "Yes . . . I . . . well . . ."

Megan: "It's your pose. Your ankles are crossed, and I can see you're looking towards the door *already, well, don't be afraid, I won't bite." *laughs* "It's fine, I see you did the test quite well!"*

Mark: "Okay" *laughs and changes pose* "Yes, I . . ."

Megan: "Was it hard, the test?"

Mark: "Well, it was kinda hard . . . but not too much. I think it was fine."

Megan: "It was fine? What did you like the most?"

Mark: "Well, the way, you know, the task was given, it was very well put . . ."

Megan: "Mark, you didn't do the test, did you? Someone else did it for you?"

Mark: "Why, no, I . . ."

Megan: "But you hold yourself well under pressure. And this is a good quality."

Mark: *takes a long pause, then exhales* "Thank you."

Megan: "I cannot recommend you as a senior specialist as of now, however, I can see you're motivated and confident. Care to try and complete a *new test here in the office, in a separate room, right now?"*

Mark: *stammers* "I . . ."

Megan: "A junior test perhaps?"

Mark: "Yes please."

Megan: "Perfect."

The difference, as you can see, is tremendous. While Susan merely questions her subject, ticking boxes off one after another, Megan is actively involved. She opens with a Barnum statement, which ends with the claim Mark feels "locked up", guarded from her . . . and she sees confirmation, quickly examining him during a short pause, no more than a glance. She sees a sign of confirmation in his locked-up posture and his new pattern of uncertain behavior, and yet his discomfort must be eased, so Megan quickly moves on to the successfully completed test.

Yet Mark doesn't act as expected, he is not relieved – he looks even more uncomfortable after the test was mentioned! This is a red flag, unpredictability of behavior.

Megan takes a step back, she asks a compassionate question – was the test hard? Mark answers with a generalized (Barnum) statement which could be applied to any test there is, not just the one he supposedly completed at home. Megan is an expert in generalized statements, and she notices it instantly. Mark is trying to *mirror* her behavior – he seeks to re-establish the lost confidence and enters this scanning mode of sorts, something we human beings often do without even realizing it, acting like the person we're talking to, copying their act in order for them to see: *I'm a friend!* And yet their instinctive part, their monkey, is watching quietly: how would this person in front of me react to themselves, what do they have to tell us about themselves, literally?

Megan recognizes not only the Barnum statement, but also the unconscious attempt of Mark's in mirroring her. She reflects it by mirroring back, echoing: "It was fine?" Mirroring back a mirrored behavior is often disorienting, because it carries a strong emotional backlash, which Megan amplifies even more by zooming in: "What did you like *the most?*"

Now Mark is obviously lying. His tone has changed, slowed down: the reason kicked in, putting a muffler on his emotions. Mark speaks slowly, picking words, *inventing* things. Megan no longer has any doubts he didn't do the test.

She asks about it directly, to put this crucial matter to rest straight off. Mark says "no", yet his intonation doesn't change, so he is technically just stalling. By now he understands his lies don't work. He is confused and likely ashamed.

Megan quickly fixes him up by admiring his confidence under stress. Mark didn't show any confidence, and this compliment has nothing to do with reality, yet confirmation bias makes Mark agree. By *agreeing* he feels confident, he accepts Megan's reality and *becomes* confident, or at least much more composed than he just was. This effect is normally called *power of suggestion,* and this is a good tool of active analysis and the emotional management of your subject.

Megan openly offers Mark to redeem himself, prove his own technical knowledge. Mark seems to agree to take the test, yet he stammers. There could be only one reason, and Megan names it: his technical skill is not enough. Instead of discouraging him from the test and discarding him, Megan decides to try and hire Mark as a junior specialist.

So, remember the active analysis sequence well: opening with a generalized (Barnum) statement to

> break the ice, then zoom in on the most obvious positive characteristic of your subject, counterweighted by cold reading and/or mirroring.

Cold reading means educated guesswork. A lot can be told about your subject from their looks, their dress, their non-verbal signals and tone, their vocabulary. Take everything relevant into account, notice every change that happens, dampen the strike with a positive statement, zoom in on important questions, and so on. If your subject seems to slow down, remember it's their reasonable personality, a less predictable and less primal one kicked in. They could be lying (they could lie on instinct as well, if the lie was prepackaged!)

Mirroring is tricky, and conscious employment of it, same as detection of the attempts of people to mirror you, takes practice. Think of it like a sonar/emitter of sorts, an intuitive device normally more developed in females than males. You take in some emotion from your subject, some impression. Transmit it back by *pretending you're them,* then analyze their response. If you want, you could specifically make them *describe you as you pose as them,* to tell you their opinion of their own character worn as a mask and presented back to them.

If you detect conscious attempts to mirror you, mimic you – the chances are the person you're communicating with belongs to the so-called dark triad: a narcissist, a sociopath, or a Machiavellian (manipulative) type. These types of people use mirroring and cognitive empathy to charm you and pretend to be a very similar, very close person to you in a way you will not be able to comprehend, in a magnetic, hypnotizing way. This bond will grant them emotional control over you, since in fact such people are not necessarily close to you in any way at all. They will often remain very cold, well-controlled, and logical, and yet you will be unable to predict their behavior. Given enough practice when looking for these features, you will be able to spot the dark triad types in conversation and take precautions against their techniques by employing your own (mirroring back).

In the next chapter, we will review the ways to employ the knowledge you obtain during analysis, and we will review both legitimate and criminal employment of analytical techniques and tricks of persuasion, to arm you against possible dark triad types or merely con artists working the same old tricks.

Because a true analyst always stays in control, as objective as possible, and must never be led astray.

9. Persuasion Basics (and Wrongs)

From ancient ages people of certain professions – merchants, diplomats, explorers – were famously employing various tricks of negotiations and persuasion. Persuasion earned money, persuasion saved lives . . . and it destroyed lives. Without persuasion, the whole religions, ideologies, and crucial historical events would simply never happen.

Or, at least it could ruin someone's payday, and this palm reading woman in the street who seemed so concerned and so knowing about Susan, telling her things about her just by the lines on her hand . . . this woman somehow managed to steal Susan's wallet, and it's like a black hole instead of the memories of their meeting in Susan's head. Was the street palmistry woman truly a magician?

So such a thing won't happen to you, we will tell you about how the street palmistry woman does it, for this is her secret criminal profession, a street hypnotist, a con.

We'll also review the work of a "telepathic" medium that makes his living performing with similar techniques onstage, and a complex business deal a certain business lady skilled in analysis and communication has to close despite multiple problems of technical and interpersonal kind.

Let's start with Susan's favorite TV Show, depicting Frank, who is a professional actor and entertainer, stage hypnotist pretending to have telepathic powers. Frank stands before the audience and says:

"They say nothing in the universe happens by accident, and it's impossible to choose someone at random. So now I will choose one of you, a volunteer, following the telepathic signal I receive from the Universe! You! Yes, you, sir!"

At this moment, the trained eyes of Frank scan the faces in the crowd and pick the first mark, a family man in his thirties, balding, seemingly shy. On hearing Frank, the man looks up, then smiles.

"What's there in your breast pocket?" Frank asks him with no pause.

"What?" The man is lost.

"There." Frank points at his breast pocket, yet the man doesn't seem to understand. This can only mean that Frank made a mistake. He expected a man would pull out a personal item, but it seems his breast pocket is empty in the end. Frank makes an impatient face.

"There, there," he repeats in quick succession, and then stops himself. "Oh, doesn't matter, thank you,

we'll ask someone else, I can see my voice already put you in a trance!"

The crowd laughs, the man sits down, and the slip is averted.

Frank points next: "You! Yes, you, sir! What's there in your trouser pocket?"

Frank doesn't actually see the man's trouser pocket. He doesn't have to see it though, as Frank now is working with statistical numbers, not with the observed evidence. The men he picks from the crowd are highly likely to carry something in the pockets he names.

The second man he named gets up and pulls out a wallet and a keyring. Frank keeps gesturing towards the wallet, motioning the man to open it. It's an automatic gesture, a part of Frank's usual routine: if *his mark pulls out a container of any kind, he motions for the container to be opened and its contents are shown. This non-verbal command of his is so well-practiced and streamlined his mark opens the wallet automatically, picks up an item, and brings it up to the cameras and the audience, so Frank can see it on the big monitor up close. It's a picture of a 3-year-old girl holding a shabby plush bunny, likely the favorite toy, judging by its condition. The girl has to be the man's daughter, still, there's a certain risk she's not. This is why Frank goes for an inclusive Barnum-shaped statement which seems intimate yet fits any little girl related to this man.*

"Yes, it's you, sir! You see, I just received a telepathic message meant for you, it seems . . . it's from your little – what's her name? Jenny! Yes, your little Jenny!" Frank says. The man merely mouthed the name for him to see, yet this could have been seen only by a few faces in the crowd. Frank's pose suggests he already started receiving the telepathic message – his eyes seem closed, his index fingers are pressed to the temples. Frank speaks into the mouthpiece in a relaxed deep voice. "She tells me to please tell you she might have left her poor . . . poor friend in the car!'"

The man didn't mouth the name of the toy, so Frank had to use a generalized statement. He quickly notices the man thought of the correct item when he heard the word "friend". Yes, it's likely his daughter, she goes everywhere with her favorite bunny toy. And so the man's amused and surprised face fills the big screen behind Frank, the audience watching the man as he is hearing Frank's words, and the look of understanding and revelation on his face is proof enough: the crowd gasps in awe at Frank's supernatural powers, and bursts into applause.

"Please come onstage," Frank invites the man, then gives him the microphone. "So your name is . . .?"

" . . .Alfred!" The man says.

"And this was your . . ."

"This is my daughter Jenny, and yes, she has this toy . . ."

"Her 'friend'?"

"Yes, a bunny by the name Thumper, and . . ."

"You . . .?" Frank gently nudges his mark towards the choices needed for the act.

"Yes, I probably left it in my car you know . . . but how did you know? About Emily, and how could you know I have a car?"

The man asks this despite the fact that in his hands, he is still holding his wallet and the keyring, with a big car alarm fab visible.

The ovation drowns out Frank's words, so the snowman merely gives the camera a smile.

Frank didn't do anything supernatural. He hardly used his attention at all, mostly trusting his trained stage reflexes. The crowd bursts into applause, and yet Frank's work had only just begun: while his audience is content, it's Frank's chance to study his mark better, and prepare his next grand revelation. The man is already impressed, and now, being in the spotlight, he's likely to submit to Frank's will and publically agree with everything Frank says about him or asks from him.

Susan loves Frank's TV show, yet it doesn't help her to understand how persuasion works, how obtained personal informational is employed on practice. Even worse, Susan's belief in supernatural makes magic possible in her world – the mundane tricks other people could find even banal will often seem like something transcending the laws of nature to Susan, making her susceptible to con artists of any kind.

During lunch, walking through a park next to her office, Susan runs into a woman wearing stark ethnical clothes, yet looking motherly and trustworthy. The woman bumps into her seemingly by accident, while Susan is distracted.

"Oh," Susan says, looking at the woman in surprise. "Oh, sorry, I . . ."

"Is the market this way, good lady?" The woman says.

"Y-yes," Susan replies. "Well, it's better to take a subway to . . ."

"Thank you so much!" The woman takes her hand. Susan wants to take it away but wavers – what if it's considered a major sign of disrespect in this exotic lady's traditions?

"Want to thank you, read your fortune on your hand, for free?" The woman suggests with a friendly smile.

Susan smiles back: "Okay."

The woman's tone and posture change radically as she steps up and turns to be faced in the same direction as Susan instead of opposing her. She grasps Susan's hand in a firm professional grip, like a masseur. She flips Susan's hand over and starts muttering to her, deep, without even tracing any lines:

"I know, my daughter, you have this secret passion deep inside, it burns you every day, you want it, but it's fickle and it avoids you, because there's a bad spell put on you by someone close to you."

Susan's head goes around, yet she takes hold of herself. She heard of some people being conned by such palm readers. They say these people can even steal all your money. And Susan has three hundred dollars cash in her wallet. She'd better keep her guard up.

"Look, I don't have any secret passion," she tells the woman, trying to take her hand away, but the woman is holding on to her. Susan says: *"You got it wrong. I'm happily married, I have two kids--"*

"At work," the woman replies momentarily. *"This is about your work."*

"Oh," Susan reconsiders what she just heard. A secret passion. Yes, she does want a coordinator's position, and then there's Megan. Susan says: *"Yes. I do have this friend back in the office. We . . . compete for a position . . ."*

"She cursed you," the woman says, looking straight into Susan's eyes without blinking. Then, as she sees Susan admits such a possibility, the woman steps in, probing her hand like a doctor who just found a very bad disease in her patient. *"Yes . . . she probably took something of yours, maybe you*

lost something recently, a hairbrush, a lipstick maybe, around your office?"

"Well, in fact I did, just the other week I lost a lipstick," Susan confirms, and then stops. How could this woman know? And Megan, she does seem a little witchy at times, she has green eyes and all. And Frank she saw on TV also warned the audience about some kind of toxic vampiric people who basically look at you wrong, and they set you up for wrong things.

Susan cannot help but remember how many wrongs happened to her in the last two months. She's distracted and disappointed. Megan, how could she do something like this to her?

"There is a cure, don't you worry," the woman tells her in a deep, warm, and sweet voice, like Susan is her little sick daughter. "We can make her curse go away!"

"We can?" Susan asks.

"You have a small coin?" The woman asks.

Automatically, Susan reaches into her purse with her clumsy left hand, the one that the palmistry woman left free. Then her right hand is finally also free, although it does feel limp after it was compressed so.

With her limp right hand, Susan slowly opens her wallet, unzips its small change compartment, and produces a fifty-cent coin.

She never thinks about the fact the wallet is left open in her left hand, as she only opened its small change compartment, and the cash is still locked in. The wallet remains in her field of vision at all times; Susan attention is concentrated on her money, and one small coin? Why not! Here are fifty cents,

Susan can spare as much. Let this woman do to the coin whatever the woman likes.

The palmistry woman makes Susan make a fist around her fifty cents. The woman grabs Susan's fist with the both of her hands and squeezes it with force, clamping Susan's hand down on the hard coin.

The woman quickly mutters an exotic spell, something in a foreign language that sounds mysterious and mind-blowing to Susan, who, like a kid on a carnival, waits for the coin to disappear.

Instead, the woman says:

"Quick, we need a small bill to wrap it in! The curse is inside that coin now! HOLD ON TO IT! HOLD ON TO IT! Don't let the curse escape again!"

She squeezes Susan's right fist very hard, making her hand cramp, and then lets go.

"Quickly, pull out a small bill! And hold to the coin, keep holding! The curse is inside the coin!" The woman's hoarse voice commands. "Need to wrap the coin in a dollar bill! Wrap the coin, quick, or bad things happen!"

Susan tries to pull out a one dollar bill while holding the coin, which now seems to burn her with its malicious curse. It's hard, but she's in control. She doesn't notice the wallet's cash compartment is now also open.

"Now wrap the coin with the small bill! Wrap the coin!" The woman quickly helps Susan make a small origami piece of the bill with the coin wrapped inside. She presses it into Susan's hand.

"Now throw the coin behind you and don't look! Throw it!" The woman commands, and Susan tosses the bill with the coin inside without thinking, and this is when a deep feeling of regret strikes her.

What is she doing now? She just let go of a dollar and fifty cents, just like that! This woman fooled her!

Susan spins back, hoping to retrieve her dollar bill before it's gone. Then she stops and turns back around.

Her wallet is in her left hand, carefully relieved of the three hundred dollars cash. Susan tries to pull out her phone with her right hand and call the police, yet her right hand is too cramped and numb even to unlock the phone, not to mention call a number. Susan is lost. It's like she's just been to some other dimension. There's no sign of the woman around. Did she even exist? What did just happen? She *cannot evaluate it. It was supernatural. She was hypnotized. Mind-controlled. Put under.*

As feelings return to her hand and she can finally call, Susan realizes she can hardly remember the woman at all. She only remembers her bright exotic clothes. There's nothing coherent she could tell the police.

Susan has got to move on, much poorer yet none wiser.

Back at work, Megan is waiting for her: they have to run a very important 2-hour presentation for the stakeholders of their current project, rebranding of a large pizzeria chain. First Susan must deliver an opening speech, then Megan will present the market research, then the stakeholders must review the history of the brand, the past solutions and their effectiveness, after which Susan and Megan will both present the new proposed solution, and then it's on to snacks, drinks, and the networking.

Susan tells Megan she cannot deliver the fifteen-minute speech in the beginning, she is distressed by an accident with the palm reading woman. Megan turns to their system administrator busy with the projector.

Megan: "Steve, will it be possible to start my part ten minutes earlier? I can deliver the opening speech, but I don't have the whole fifteen minutes of material, I will only take about five, ten minutes at best."

Steven: "That's a problem."

Megan: "Why?"

Steven: "Well, because it TURNS OUT our conference room laptop DIED, and I ONLY found out about it this MORNING when I tried to switch it on. Someone must have spilled WATER on it, and told NO ONE. I brought my OWN laptop, but it's a MAC, and it turns out we don't have the proper connector, SO."

Megan: "Will we be able to start in fifteen minutes as planned?"

Steven: "There's a chance, but I cannot say yet. I'll try to make the connector we need out of two or three other connectors, but it may HAPPEN it just won't WORK. Then I'll have to go out and buy it, which will take about an hour."

Megan: "An hour!"

Steven: "What can I DO, Meg? It's an EMERGENCY. We couldn't KNOW it will happen, so I'm not prepared to deal with it in MINUTES."

Megan: "We cannot cancel this meeting. It may bury the whole project."

Steven: "Not MY problem."

Megan's next impulse is to strike back and reprimand Steve in front of everyone present. How is it not his problem? The reputation of their company is at stake. She could say a lot about Steven's attitude right now.

Megan is a well-trained businesswoman though. She programmed herself to react to every impulse of aggression, which she perceives as red fog descending on her, with mental freeze, followed by a gradual, cold, and restrained analysis of the situation.

If she starts a scene now, she won't make things any better. She only could have made them worse, much worse, throwing accusations around in front of every stakeholder of her project. Right now, as never before, they all must be as strong as they can in terms of teamwork and connection. She hates Steve merely because he informed her of a problem, attacking the messenger. This was something he didn't cause and couldn't have prevented. He is also extremely upset by what happened, which shows. It must be because he will have to spend half a monthly budget of his department just to replace the dead laptop in their conference room. Her current issue is indeed hers to solve, not his. He was right. She was wrong. After employing common sense and reviewing the situation slowly, Megan is able to dismantle and dissipate a negative emotion threatening not only her current situation, but her entire career – who knows what would happen if she let go and started screaming at Steve, the way she felt like doing at first?

"You're right," she tells Steven. He is surprised yet happy to hear it. Their team connection was just cemented by her, not destroyed and then rationalized somehow by her reason, late to the party as it ever is, explaining her actions to her in retrospective: "I was angry, and he shouldn't have

crossed me. He said it wasn't his problem, how the hell wasn't it his problem?"

Megan made the right choice, more beneficial to her. Knowing her own personality, she was wise to put such a "mental firewall" between her aggression and the blood sacrifices it demands.

Now she could make a ten-minute opening speech, and then show her slides and diagrams . . . soon her intuition tells her of another problem. She pulls out her portable hard drive.

"Will this thing work with your Mac laptop?" She asks Steven. He gives the hard drive a brief glance, then shakes his head. It won't. She won't be able to run their market research presentation, either.

"Could you just go buy a new PC laptop, straight off, without wasting time with these connectors?" She asks.

"Well, if I leave NOW, won't be back for the next hour and a half," Steven says. "It takes at least THIS long to sign the warranty forms and fill in all the other paperwork."

Megan has to solve this problem. They do fit within their conference room reservation time; they'll have the room for three more hours, because Megan was supposed to arrange snacks and drinks afterward, so the stakeholders would have a chance to network. Susan has the budget for the snacks, so perhaps Megan could serve them upfront, stall the stakeholders, and save the day?

"Suze, we need to open our event with the buffet hour," she whispers to Susan. "You have those three hundred bucks on you?"

Susan pales. She mutters something about how someone just stole the money from her, in a park during their lunch break. Megan can hardly understand the details, but she does realize their snack money is gone. Susan and she must be really down on their luck today.

Megan's impulse is to despair, call the event off, and perhaps lose the client. What could she do? There's nothing that could be done now. Their presentation was doomed from the start. She may as well accept it, submit to the outrageous fortune.

Yet her alarm goes off again. Go cold and restrained. Use common sense. Nothing can be done? No way to save them? Here's the client in front of her, who owns a pizzeria chain. What're three hundred bucks to him?

She approaches the client and smiles at him.

"Excuse me, Mr. Smith, may I ask something? Thank you."

Megan steps closer, draws her client's attention to herself, and speaks fast, in a tone of a conspiring friend:

"I just had this idea: why don't we open with a buffet hour instead of closing with it? And more, we could use this opportunity to introduce them to your product, make them try your wonderful pizzas before they get to decide on their future, right? What do you say?"

"Well . . ." Mr. Smith looks pleased. "I think this is a good idea."

"How fast could you get us your delivery van here?"

Her client looks concerned.

"Is ten minutes fine with you?" He asks. "I wish you told me earlier. I'd make a call right now."

"Please!" Megan smiles at him again. "I'll entertain our guests in the meantime."

Ten minutes is perfectly fine, as she needs as much for her opening speech. Then they're going to have a nice pizza party, while Steven replaces the conference room laptop. Their presentation is saved.

This is a happy ending even for Susan, who lost nothing in the end, as their snacks and drinks were sponsored by the client, who didn't mind at all.

Still, Susan is none wiser, while Megan developed a new business strategy.

This is about the only way to show to you how persuasion works, and how an active, a proactive analyst may not only work with their subjects to obtain personal knowledge about them, but also establish positive communication with them, which ends in strengthening social and business connections for common benefit of everyone involved, a mindful act with no casualties and no burnt bridges.

10. Afterword

We will not lie to you and pretend there is some kind of social justice, or universal justice, ruling over this Earth. The world we live in is unfair, and it's easy to succeed in life being a dishonest, treacherous, Machiavellian type of person, for whom their personal gain justifies any sort of means.

These people exist. They do succeed. They become major power figures and rule the world. They change the way our planet works, they start wars and establish religions. They kill or rob millions of people in the process. They die rich, happy, and successful, in their beds, one hundred and something years old. This is how it was before, and this is how it is now, and we cannot be blind to the facts of it.

This doesn't mean however that this is how it should be. If only honest people, kind and mindful people, who care about what happens to the humankind as a whole, who sincerely wish everyone around them nothing but the best – if only these people were as well versed in analysis and persuasion as the dishonest and selfish types!

The problem is honesty is an artificial construct. Full objectivity hardly exists when we talk about human character. We often lie for good causes, and never worry about us doing something bad by doing so. We easily circumvent and override our conscience when we need to. To many of us, deep inside, social norms and morals hardly mean anything at all – only the *peer pressure* matters to us, the fact that, *if people around us knew,* they'd shun us and hate us, or even lock us up for our actions.

But if no one will ever know, is there really anything that stops us? Anything our reason will not be able to dismantle, neutralize, rationalize and make go away? It only takes a desire strong enough to overrule the will, or catch us unawares, we will temporarily aligned with our primal needs, our common sense left out as it happens.

This is why, instead of conscience, we appeal to your honor.

The modern culture is much more peaceful, more reasonable than it used to be. We – or at least the most of us – no longer think in terms of sin and virtue. We do not deprive ourselves of pleasures for ritualistic, spiritual reasons; at least we no longer do it with fervor and zeal that could once destroy a family or consume a life. We accept our basic desires – catering to one's flesh, seeking the life of luxury is no longer morally questionable or detestable in our world.

Every medal has two sides however. The present human society, speaking equally of the Western and the Eastern society, seems to value ego above everything else; "being oneself", "being special", "staying true to one's inner nature", and "listening to one's heart" becoming the staples of the quest for happiness, which is the ultimate goal of our universal culture. We fail to notice this, but in the present times, we seem to serve a golden calf of our 'self-esteem' and 'self-worth' with the zeal we used to reserve for witch burnings, and we suffer, and make other people suffer, seeking an unobtainable state called "high enough self-esteem".

This is because the true key to personal happiness doesn't lie in catering to the primal urges, same as it doesn't lie in disabling or suppressing them, as many religions tend to claim. The happiness hides in balance between the desires of the flesh and those of the mind, our reason – the chatty computer – being employed as a tool to seek solutions to the problems plaguing our monkey, and not vice versa.

Too many people live their life on instinct alone, repeating a simple routine and compensating for the lack of free will with "spiritual" introspection, which yields them nothing except for occasional bouts of grandiose sense of self-worth. Too many people use their reason to explain their actions to themselves *after* they act, without employing common sense beforehand at all. Their couch potato of a brain is watching their life in retrospective, after it's already happened, and tells them why it all had to be so.

The main goal of this book is to teach you to do otherwise. Observe, analyze, and then act. Satisfy your mind, and then cater to your body. Switch on the computer and click its mental keys a bit before the monkey decides what to do.

And this is when you will understand our life doesn't have to be a rat race, a Darwinian battle of primates for status, for food and shelter, for the praise of opposite sex (or the same sex). Instead, we could be attentive, helpful, and mindful towards each other, connect and grow strong instead of falling divided. None of us has to be lonely, shunned by others for an unknown reason, and ashamed of themselves. Our common sense always prevails in the end . . . the problem is it often prevails when it's too late.

And this is about the only thing that stands between us, human beings, and our personal happiness, which then adds up to our common good.

We will be happy if this book brings you one step closer to this vision.

11. Disclaimer

The information contained in **"The Art Of Reading People"** and its components, is meant to serve as a comprehensive collection of strategies that the author of this eBook has done research about. Summaries, strategies, tips and tricks are only recommendations by the author, and reading this eBook will not guarantee that one's results will exactly mirror the author's results.

The author of this Ebook has made all reasonable efforts to provide current and accurate information for the readers of this eBook. The author and its associates will not be held liable for any unintentional errors or omissions that may be found.

The material in the Ebook may include information by third parties. Third party materials comprise of opinions expressed by their owners. As such, the author of this eBook does not assume responsibility or liability for any third party material or opinions.

The publication of third party material does not constitute the author's guarantee of any information, products, services, or opinions contained within third party material. Use of third party material does not guarantee that your results will mirror our results. Publication of such third party material is simply a recommendation and expression of the author's own opinion of that material.

Whether because of the progression of the Internet, or the unforeseen changes in company policy and editorial submission guidelines, what is stated as fact at the time of this writing may become outdated or inapplicable later.

This Ebook is copyright ©2018 by **Richard Martinez** with all rights reserved. It is illegal to redistribute, copy, or create derivative works from this Ebook whole or in parts. No parts of this report may be reproduced or retransmitted in any forms whatsoever without the written expressed and signed permission from the author.

This self-help book is very experimental in nature. We never bothered you with references to other books and studies so far, because we didn't want to distract you from the reading. Below you will find the list of recommended reads related to people analysis, and the psychology and neurophysiology involved.

12. Recommended Reading

Erich Fromm "The Art of Listening"

Erich Fromm "Escape from Freedom" ("The Fear of Freedom")

Daniel Kahneman "Thinking, Fast and Slow"

David Rock "Your Brain at Work"

Eric Berne "Games People Play: The Psychology of Human Relationships"

Tania Singer "Caring Economics: Conversations on Altruism and Compassion, Between Scientists, Economists, and the Dalai Lama"

Konstantin Stanislawski "Method of Physical Action"

Andrew Bradbury "Develop Your NLP Skills"

Christian Keysers "The Empathic Brain", "Mirror Neurons"

Made in the USA
San Bernardino, CA
29 January 2020

63741042R00068